Get Set Go Phonics

The Princess and the Pea

Phonics Consultant Susan Purcell
Illustrator Charlotte Cooke
Concept Fran Bromage

Miles Kelly

Once upon a time, there was a proud prince, who lived a happy life in a creepy old castle, but he was a bit lonely.

I wish I could meet a princess.

I promise we'll find you a princess.

Say the words as you spot each thing in the picture.

prince

crown

creepers

2

One day, the prince's father, the king, cried, "Let's cross our country and find you a princess."

Sound out these words, which all use the **cr** and **pr** blends.

crab   crow   crunch   cry

price   press   pretty

The family stayed in some great palaces.

Princesses came from near and far, aiming to impress the waiting prince.

Say the names of the things in the picture as you spot them. They all use the **ai** sound.

waiter   plate   face   cake

Mostly, the princesses behaved well, but some were vain, some were lazy and some just wanted the cake!

Spot the word that doesn't use the **ai** sound.

stay   play   grand   train

The prince did meet a lovely princess called Julia, who seemed just right.

But sadly Julia told terrible jokes, was jumpy and jittery and couldn't sit still! She just wouldn't do either!

Find something in the picture that begins with j.

Sound out these words with the j sound.

job jelly jumper join

giraffe giant gentle

The prince returned to his faraway castle feeling sad.

One night there was a fearsome storm. Fierce lightning lit up the sky. It was so cold that everyone stayed close by the fire.

Say the words as you spot things with the f sound in the picture.

fire

fur

feet

7

In the middle of the night, there was a loud knocking at the door.

It was such a nasty night, the queen felt nervous about the noise.

Spot the word that doesn't begin with the n sound.

neck   meal   knit   knee

When they heard the knocking again they opened the door.

There stood a girl with dripping wet, curly hair.

Point out the ur sound (as in curly)

Sound out these words, which all use the **ur** sound.

learn   search   stir   bird

turn   nurse   purple

Draw attention to the **air** sound (as in h**air**)

The king invited the girl in. He gave her a ch**air** by the fire, so she could dry her h**air**.

The prince couldn't help but st**are** at her.

Sound out these words with the **air** sound.

fair   pair   share   square

bear   wear   there

Emphasize the m sound (as in mug)

The girl sipped a mug of warm milk, and tried not to make a mess on the carpet.

Spot the word that doesn't use the **m** sound.

mat   net   mud   mix   mop

Highlight the oo sound (as in soon)

Soon, the girl grew warm and dry. Now she was in a much better mood.

"Who ARE you?" asked the prince. The girl told him she was a princess!

Spot the word that doesn't have the oo sound.

chew   group   blue   coat

The queen didn't believe this.

"Let's prepare a room and prove whether she is a true princess," thought the queen.

Sound out some more words with the **oo** sound.

moon   roof   clue   glue

soup   move   fruit

13

As the maids began to make the girl's bed, the queen balanced a pea on the bottom of the bedstead.

Say the words as you spot things with the b sound in the picture.

14

bed

banner

bow

"She will have a beastly night's sleep if she is a real princess," said the queen, "because she will feel a big lump in the bed!"

Spot the word that doesn't use the **b** sound.

back   bird   duck   bend

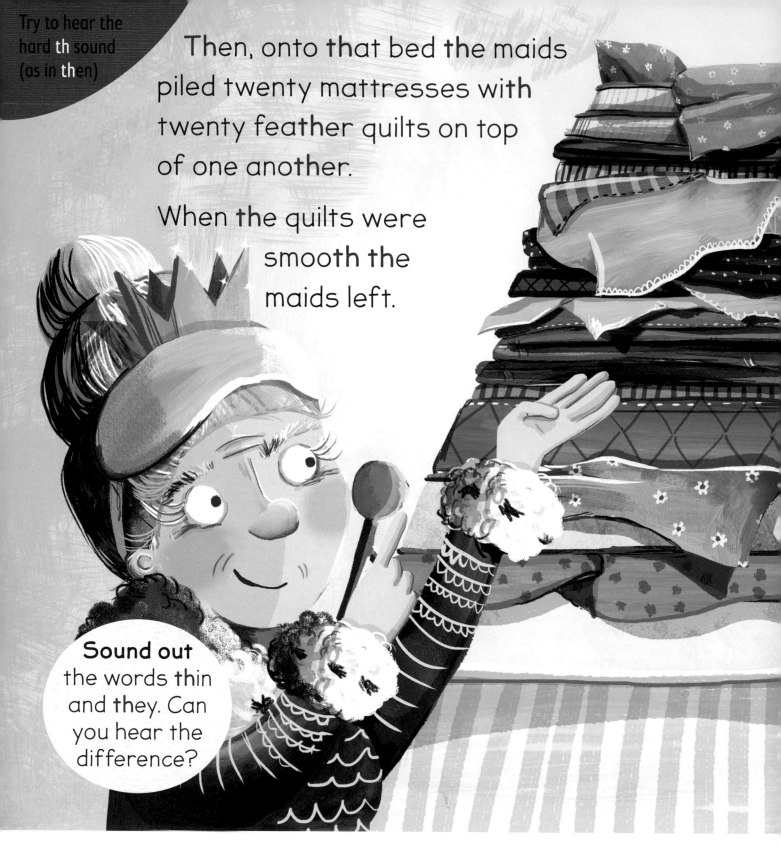

Try to hear the hard th sound (as in then)

Then, onto that bed the maids piled twenty mattresses with twenty feather quilts on top of one another.

When the quilts were smooth the maids left.

Sound out the words thin and they. Can you hear the difference?

Sound out some words with the hard th sound.

these   those   other
weather   brother   rather

The prince's mother fetched the girl from the other room and there she was left for the night.

Spot the word that doesn't use the hard **th** sound.

this   there   father   shirt

In the morning, the queen swept into the girl's room. "Tell me, how did you sleep?" she asked.

The girl could barely speak. "I'm so tired, I could weep," she squeaked.

Spot the word that doesn't use the **ee** sound.

sheet   tree   dress   meat

As you read, emphasize the bl blend

"I didn't sleep at all," the girl blurted out. "There was a lump under the blankets. I'm black and blue all over!"

Sound out some words with the **bl** blend.

blast   blend   block   blink

blow   blunt   bless

Emphasize the ow sound (as in now)

There was no doubt about the girl now. Only a princess would have felt a little round pea in the bed.

When the prince found out, he gave a shout of joy.

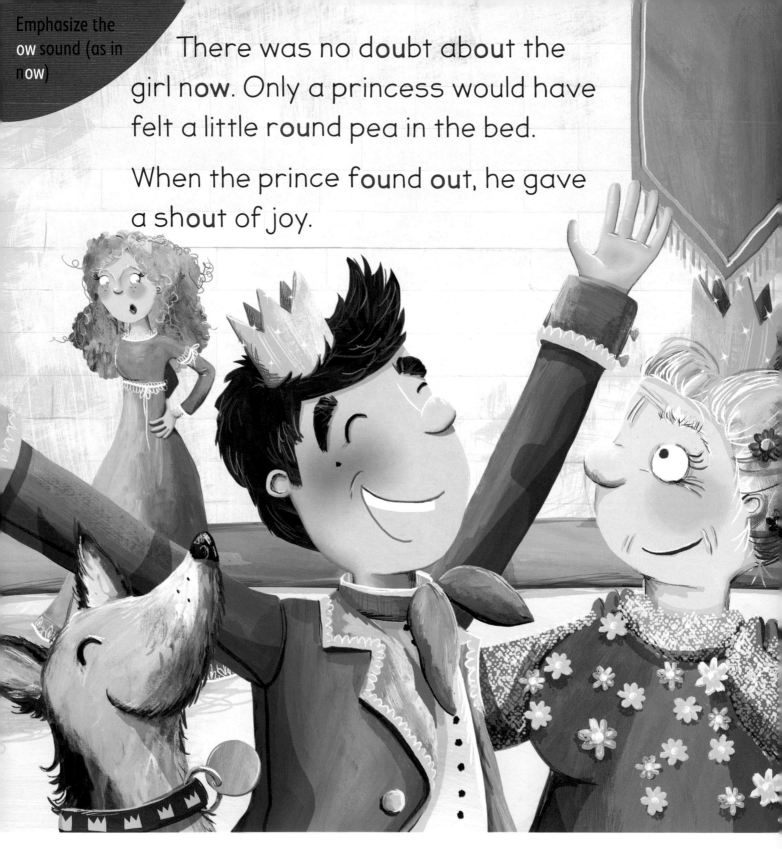

Emphasize the **ow** sound as you say this sentence together.

When the prince found out, he gave a shout of joy.

The prince **vow**ed to marry the princess, and ast**ou**nded her by asking her right away. They didn't hang ab**ou**t!

Can you **point** to something in the picture that has the **ow** sound?

Sound out some more words with the **ow** sound.

cow   brown   town
ground   mouth   amount

And what do you think happened to that special little pea?

It was placed in the royal museum – where it probably still is today.

Spot the word that doesn't use the **t** sound.

team   wolf   boot   part

Ask your child to **retell** the story using these key sounds and story images.

prince

waiting

night

girl

stare

true

bed

sleep

vowed

creepy   crow   crab   cry

giant   jelly   gentle   just

fur   feeling   fierce   fire

heard   curly   bird   turn

mug   mix   mess   milk

blue   roof   true   soup

they   rather   with   then

blow   blanket   blink   black

today   team   boot   part

You've had fun with phonics! Well done.